# BASIC ESSENTIALS™
# RAFTING

# Help Us Keep This Guide Up to Date

Every effort has been made by the author and editors to make this guide as accurate and useful as possible. However, many things can change after a guide is published—new products and information become available, regulations change, techniques evolve, etc.

We would love to hear from you concerning your experiences with this guide and how you feel it could be improved and be kept up to date. While we may not be able to respond to all comments and suggestions, we'll take them to heart and we'll also make certain to share them with the author. Please send your comments and suggestions to the following address:

The Globe Pequot Press
Reader Response/Editorial Department
P.O. Box 480
Guilford, CT 06437

Or you may e-mail us at:

editorial@globe-pequot.com

Thanks for your input.

# BASIC ✷ ESSENTIALS™

# RAFTING

## SECOND EDITION

## BY JIB ELLISON

The Globe Pequot Press

Guilford, Connecticut

*To Bill McGinnis, Jim Cassady, and*
*Mike Grant-Whitewater*
*Cowboys all.*

Cover photo by Paul Gallaher/Index Stock Imagery
Cover design by Lana Mullen
Text and layout design by Casey Shain
Interior photos ©Michael R.Speaks, Denali Park

**Library of Congress Cataloging-in-Publication Data**

Ellison, Jib.
    Basic essentials. Rafting/by Jib Ellison.—2nd ed.
       p. cm. —(Basic essentials series)
    Rev. ed. of:The basic essentials of rafting. c1991.
    Includes index.
    ISBN 0-7627-0665-1
       1. Rafting (Sports) I. Ellison, Jib. Basic essentials of rafting. II. Title.
GV780.E46 2000
797.1'21—dc21                                     00-035385

Manufactured in the United States of America
Second Edition/First Printing

# Contents

# ON THE RIVER

The sound is unmistakable. Like a lion's roar, the rapid warns that it lies in wait—just downstream. The spring sun filters through the tall pine trees, their smell mixed with the bite of thin mountain air. Although your heart is racing, you feel strangely calm. Time seems to move slowly. Butterflies flutter about in your stomach. You yawn, although sleep is the furthest thing from your mind. This is the proverbial calm before the storm.

The noise is deafening now. You have to scream loudly in order for your team of paddlers to hear you. Although you're almost on top of the churning rapid, you still cannot see downstream below the horizon line. You stand. Your entire being is focused on the rapid ahead. Rocks and waves and chaotic white foaming water are everywhere. Suddenly you see the route through the maelstrom and call a command, "Forward!" As one, your crew responds and the boat lunges into the rapid.

An unexpected wave hits the bow and slaps the raft sideways. "Left turn!" you scream, trying to regain control and get the raft back on course. Some of the crew hear you, others don't. You holler the command again, this time with more urgency. A house-size boulder lies downstream. Just seconds ago it looked far away. Now it looms big. The boat broaches and begins to wrap around the rock. You call "rock slide!" and this time everyone knows what to do. Your crew scrambles to the high side of the raft, and their quick reaction prevents the raft from flipping. The raft peels off the rock and goes over a small ledge into a hole. The impact sends two of the crew into the river. Bobbing like corks in their lifejackets, they come up right next to the boat and you reach over and pull them quickly back into the raft.

But the rapid isn't over.

No time to think about what went wrong; only time to choose where to go from here. Looking downstream, you decide on a new route, and call another command. "Right turn!" you scream. The response is quick and turns the boat into the next wave. Suddenly you're in control again. Another rock lies ahead, but this time you

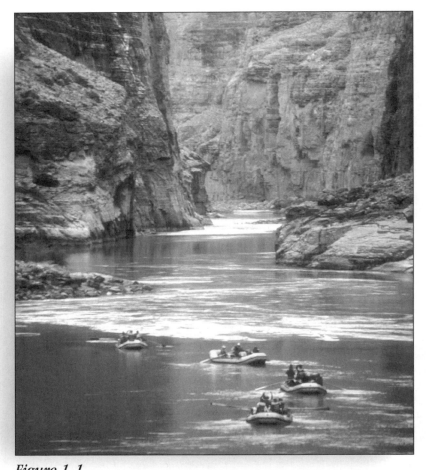

*Figure 1-1*

**Rafts floating a peaceful stretch of the Colorado**

*Figure 1-2*

**An oar boat on a river in Pakistan**

avoid it easily. Next thing you know you're at the bottom, in the calm pool, wet and exhilarated. Everyone lets out a cheer. You have experienced life to its fullest.

This book outlines the basic essentials of rafting. When used in conjunction with a hands-on training program or to supplement a commercial trip, it can assist you in learning rafting skills quickly and safely. Soon you'll plunge into the depths of this exciting new sport that brings you face to face with the forces of nature. For now, go run a hot bath, climb in, splash around, get wet, and read on. I'll see you downstream!

# BOATS, BOATS, BOATS

There are almost as many different kinds of boats as there are rivers to float. Inflatable, plastic, Hypalon, high-tech, duct-taped, Lexatron, big, small, squat, and sleek-raft designs of today integrate spaceship engineering, explorer tradition, and down-home ingenuity. But no matter what boat you choose to explore the river corridors of our wondrous planet, with forethought, prudence, and enthusiasm your journey will be safe and fun.

## Raft History

Recreational rafting in the United States began in earnest after World War II. War-related innovations in materials, design, and glue produced durable assault boats and life rafts, which were later salvaged and used on rivers. Until recently, you could see the original Navy "basket boats"—soft circular boats that when inflated looked like bulbous baskets—careening down easy rivers with drenched, smiling, and clueless occupants.

In the 1950s, as the sport grew more popular, the quality of rafts improved. Newly formed whitewater outfitting companies realized that the military boat supply was limited and began to manufacture their own boats. The specialized needs of the outfitters helped to elevate the quality of raft design and material to a higher level. They needed boats that were able to safely handle more people and gear. Designers and engineers bitten by the whitewater bug modified the old basket boats to withstand tougher whitewater conditions. Up-turned bows and sterns made of stiffer, more durable materials were developed. By the mid-1970s rafts designed specifically for whitewater rivers flooded the market, but they came with an odd hold over from the "basket boats"—they filled up with water.

## Bathtub Boats

Although materials and designs had improved, the majority of rafts still had sealed floors, which held water like a bathtub. The exception to this rule was the large motor-driven pontoon rafts used to run the large-volume rivers of the American Southwest. But for most rafters, throughout the 1970s and 1980s they had no choice but to bail.

It was a simple task.

After a challenging wet rapid, a crew member would unleash a large pickle bucket, then commence bailing tons of water out of the raft back into the river. This was the only option if you wanted to go rafting.

Many a sad tale has been told about the nightmares of losing the bailing bucket in the middle of a big rapid. Without the ability to be bailed, the raft became very heavy and sluggish, making stopping and maneuvering difficult, if not impossible. This limitation made difficult rivers the exclusive domain of kayakers for many years, simply because water couldn't be bailed out of a raft fast enough to compensate for the water coming in.

Bailing became part of the experience, and techniques were invented accordingly. People learned how to run rapids "dry"— avoiding all but the unavoidable waves. Often one of the crew was designed as the "swamper" whose main responsibility was to bail. Regardless of the inconvenience of having to bail, bailing boats were and still are more than adequate for the vast majority of runnable rivers in the world.

Today the advantages to standard bailing rafts are price and the fact that, for all but the most difficult rivers, a self-bailer isn't necessary. Also, the bailing raft's main disadvantage—the fact that tons of water must be bailed out of the raft after every rapid—can sometimes become a major advantage: The pickle bucket is a key element for a successful water fight with other boaters.

## Self-Bailing Rafts

In the United States, early attempts at self-bailing designs failed for the most part. In one attempt, rafters removed the floors and laced noninflatable floors to the side tubes. In another, they removed the floors altogether and hung wooden decks as floors. Neither of these designs worked very well. Instead of draining water out of the raft, these floors often sunk under the surface of the water—rendering would-be self-bailers practically useless. Nonetheless, everyone kept searching for the design that would allow freedom from the pickle bucket.

In 1983 the first working self-bailing prototype was developed by Jim Cassady in conjunction with Whitewater Manufacturing. The secret to its success was an inflatable floor (Figure 2-1). All earlier attempts at designing self-bailers had neglected this crucial feature. The inflatable floor rode high above the surface of the river. Any water inside the boat drained out through grommets, which attached the floor to the side tubes. In all, it was an elegant solution, and with new innovations in material and gluing technique, it did the job.

It is amazing that it took American rafters until the 1980s to figure out that self-bailing boats were the only reasonable answer to rafting difficult rivers where the gradient was steep and the volume big.

*Figure 2-1*
........................
**A self-bailing inflatable floor**

*Figure 2-2*

**Wing inflatables, a new breed of self-bailing rafts**

When exploring the Katun River in Siberia in 1988, I met a gregarious group of Russian river runners. They invited us into their tents for vodka and saltpork, shared their tall whitewater tales, then shyly explained that while our boats were well made, perhaps we should consider "to maybe cut out floor." They could not imagine any benefit derived from a non-self-bailer. A boat that fills up with water doesn't make much sense on steep Siberian rivers. We agreed and drank a toast to international friendship, but left the floor in place.

The advantages of the self-bailing raft (Figure 2-2) make it the boat of the twenty-first century. However, on a vast majority of popular, relatively easy runs in the United States, guiding a self-bailing raft down the river can be like driving a Porsche in rush-hour traffic: exhilarating, but somewhat frustrating. Like a high-performance car, the stunning maneuverability of a self-bailer can be best appreciated while "driving" on a challenging course rather than an easy one.

With the advent of better materials and self-bailing rafts, whitewater has become increasingly more accessible to a greater number of people.

# Catarafts

Russian river runners were smart. Unlike American river runners, who started rafting in basket boats and then invented new designs based on the original theme, Russians designed whitewater boats from a different starting point. Teams of geologists coming home after months in the taiga decided to float rather than walk out of the wilderness. What kind of boat would work best on the region's steep, powerful rivers? A bailing boat was out of the question. No time to stop to bail. Besides, finding pickle buckets in the middle of Siberia was not an easy task.

What the Russian geologists eventually came up with is the cataraft (Figure 2-3). The design is simple. Similar in structure to catamarans used for sailing in the West, Russian catarafts look like two parallel, cigar-shaped tubes lashed to a frame. These handmade catarafts are constructed by Russian rafting enthusiasts with whatever materials are available, such as truck tire innertubes, nylon shells, and frames made from deadwood birch boughs. Best of all, these

*Figure 2-3*

**A Russian cataraft**

# RAFT RACING

Is it possible to race these bulbous crafts? Yes, it is, and it's a sport that is growing in popularity. Already developed and respected in Europe as a competitive activity, raft racing is gaining momentum in the United States.

Rafting competitions are usually composed of three components—slalom, sprint, and downriver races. In a slalom race there are seven to ten gates suspended throughout Class II–V whitewater. The paddlers must maneuver through the gates without touching a pole. A five-second penalty is incurred if the boat or a paddler touches a pole, and a fifty-second penalty is incurred if the gate is missed or all members of the team are not inside the gate as the boat passes through it. The sprint is usually ½ mile long through a Class IV or V rapid and has a head-to-head start, with two boats starting at once. If the two teams are well suited for each other, they aggressively jockey for position throughout the entire rapid. The downriver race is the most grueling, as it entails paddling hard downstream for 6 to15 kilometers through Class IV and V whitewater. The start is often Le Mans, making for some exciting action at the beginning.

All racing is exciting, and raft racing is a great way to practice communication and teamwork while working out together in a boat. If you would like to learn more about how to be involved, call Rapid Pulse (650-347-7230), or visit their Web site at www.rapidpulse.net.

—Beth Rypins, captain, U.S. Women's Whitewater Team

catamarans are engineered to fit neatly inside a backpack for a 100-kilometer march to put-in—a journey that is necessary to reach the isolated banks of many Russian rivers.

The cataraft is now the premier whitewater raft race boat throughout the world. Light, swift, and agile, the cataraft is only out-maneuvered by decked kayaks and canoes. In the Nantahala World Whitewater Rafting Championship, two- and four-person catarafts competed in slalom and grand slalom events. At the Chuya Rally held every year in the Altai Mountains in Siberia, over fifty different types of catarafts are raced in the events. However, whitewater enthusiasts around the world are combining state-of-the-art rafting materials with Russian engineering concepts to create a new generation of supercats—capable of feats that were unimaginable several years ago.

Catarafts can be propelled either by paddles or by oars. In Russia, catarafts are used exclusively as paddle boats. Here in the United States, catarafts have been used primarily as oar boats. Which is better? Neither. They're just different. Different strokes for different folks. But no matter how you rig it, catarafts are high on the wave of the future in whitewater rafting.

## Other Boats

Bailing, self-bailing, and catarafts are only a few of the many types of "floatable people propellants" used today on whitewater rivers. In the Grand Canyon of the Colorado River, big "J" and "snout" rigs powered by huge oars and gas engines carry up to thirty people at a time through crashing rapids, and sleek wooden dories (Figure 2-4) have been modified with stronger hulls and upturned bows for the Colorado's powerful whitewater. Kayaks and canoes routinely run every sort of river, from the placid to the ridiculous. Huge, stable "plohts" and "checksters" with their long sweep oars routinely career down the glacial rivers of Eastern European mountains. Even surfing "boogie boards" have recently been enlarged to meet the rigors of river running.

*Figure 2-4*
...........................
**A dory rides the waters of Lava Falls in Colorado**

# Paddle Boats

Paddle boats (Figure 2-5) are very popular in the United States. Each summer, thousands of people make the pilgrimage to rivers throughout the country. There they are met by a guide, handed a paddle, shown a seat on the boat, and told to go "Forward!" Paddle boats utilize the combined efforts of the entire crew or team to maneuver through the rapids. Everyone paddles, everyone is involved.

Paddles move the boat around. A good whitewater paddle should be stout, from 3 to 5 feet long and have a large blade. The best paddles also have a T-shaped grip.

Paddle boats come in many sizes, from 4 feet to 20 feet in length, and can accommodate from 3 to 12 people. Each member of the paddle team sits on the side tubes. The guide usually sits in back and uses verbal commands to direct the crew's actions. Lithe and maneuverable, paddle boats rely mostly on good teamwork as opposed to brute strength for success. The river does most of the work, so that on all but the most difficult rivers, you need not have superhuman strength to safely paddle a river.

*Figure 2-5*
..........................
**Fully-loaded expedition paddle boats**

First thing to do is to go on a commercially outfitted trip. For a fee, the outfitter will provide all of the specialty gear and necessary expertise to make your journey safe and fun. This way you can get your feet wet before jumping in all the way.

Once you're hooked, you'll want to do it yourself. Here is a list of some of the basics and what you can expect to pay:

**PADDLE BOAT RIG**
Self-bailing raft $2,000-$4,000
Paddles $50-$150 each
Lifejacket $100-$200 each
Helmets $40-$150 each
First-aid kit $100
Repair $100
Throw rope $75
Pump $100-$200
Waterproof bags/boxes $100-$300 each

**OAR BOAT RIG add:**
Frame $300-$1,000
Oars (set of 3) $150-$300 each
Straps $25

# Oar Boats

Oar boats (Figure 2-6) are the workhorses of the whitewater world. It is quite normal to see a big oar boat piled high with gear being rowed through an even bigger rapid by a very small person. Oar boats look like inflatable versions of the stereotypical rowboats everyone used to take out on the lake. An oar guide uses a pair of stout oars to steer, pull, and push the raft around shifting currents and through thundering holes. These oars are usually between 8 and 12 feet long and have to be strong to withstand the rigors of whitewater rafting. The oars are attached to a frame, which is lashed to the raft. The guide sits high on a slant board seat and enjoys a great deal of autonomy in choosing and executing where to take the raft.

There is more equipment associated with outfitting and rigging an oar boat such as a frame, oars, and a rowing seat. On multiday river trips, it is the oar boats that usually carry the majority of gear. For this reason, it is often more time-consuming to rig an oar boat than a paddle boat due to the amount of bags, boxes, coolers, and the like that must be securely fastened onto the oar boat.

Both means of rafting have their advantages: In a paddle boat everyone in the crew participates in maneuvering the raft down the river, while in an oar boat the captain at the oars has total control and rows alone on a more solo type of adventure. But either way, the net result is the same—fun!

No matter how you do it, river running is a wonderful adventure. Rafting happens to be one of the most flexible, inclusive, and versatile ways to visit the magical places through which mountain rivers flow. Now that we know what the boats look like, let's find out what the rivers themselves look like.

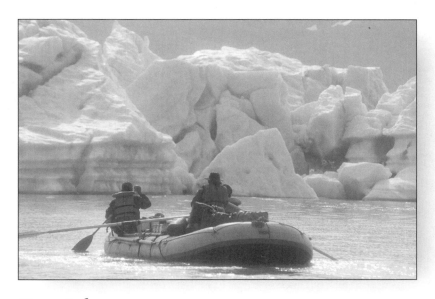

*Figure 2-6*

**An oar-powered raft using oarlocks and paddlers**

# WHITEWATER!

**3**

hat makes that sleepy rolling river that Huck Finn floated down turn into a raging torrent? What geologic anomaly compels calm, meandering water to explode into a churning, boiling, blasting rapid? What turns a serene river into a frenzied cascade?

In this chapter we will explore some of the less metaphysical answers to these questions. My hope is that you will begin to get a feel for the forces that make whitewater (Figures 3-1 and 3-2) what it is—white, wild, and fun!

You will know when a rapid is approaching. Usually you will hear what sounds like a distant train downstream. Not too much to think about really, until the realization strikes that the nearest railroad is many miles away. The thundering grows louder. Looking ahead, the river seems to disappear, plunging out of sight. The "horizon line," that point in a river where the water's surface and the sky appear to meet, is close and getting closer. The rapid approaches. The whitewater waits. Huck, what do we do?

## Rapids

Rapids are caused by three main factors: volume, gradient, and obstacles. The volume of water in a river refers to the amount of water present—from a trickle to a torrent. The gradient refers to the drop of the river over some specified distance. Obstacles are those things that inhibit or constrict the river's flow. The higher the volume, the steeper the gradient, the more the obstacles, the bigger the rapids. For example, a high volume of water dropping steeply

*Figure 3-1*

**Heavy whitewater on the Bio Bio River in Chile**

*Figure 3-2*

**Rafters on the Colorado River in the Grand Canyon**

## HIGH WATER CAMPING

September 14, 1994. Katmandu, Nepal. The monsoon rains were slow to recede, and the Sun Kosi, Nepal's River of Gold, was still flowing a fat 100,000 cfs, about five times the average flow of the Grand Canyon. On the way to put-in, a soft, warm rain kept us company as we inflated rafts, rigged gear, and finally pushed off downriver late due to a slow start from town. As dusk fell, we landed on a big sandbank island, only about 12 inches above river level. Most of us were a little skeptical, but we all said, "Great camp," not wanting to double guess the trip leader, Rocky Fairchild, on his first river decision. So we went for it, made camp, toasted the river gods, and as pitch-black night fell upon us, hit the hay.

The drizzle never let up. At midnight the river began rising quickly. My partner, Marc Goddard, being the farthest upstream, was the first to have 3 inches of water flowing through his tent. The torrent woke Marc's fiancee, Damara. She said, "Honey, is it normal to have this much water in the tent?" In a sleepy stupor he stuck his head out of the tent and saw that the river was invading our island. He yelled in a broken voice, "WATER!!!" We all woke in a panic and in the pitch darkness broke camp as if a tornado had hit it and floated our rafts and gear across the ever-growing channel that was separating us from the mainland, which was a steep jungle bank. Seeing our headlamps scurrying all over the beach was like a surrealistic scene performed by an avant-garde dance troupe. We all safely made it to the mainland and huddled the rest of the night under a big banana leaf plant until dawn broke and showed our shocked faces. The expressions told how we had learned the vital lesson to never camp on a sinking island in the rainy season!

—Lawerence Alvarez Roos, cofounder, Bio Bio Expeditions

through a narrow, boulder-choked gorge results in a powerful rapid filled with whitewater. In contrast, a small-volume river trickling through a flat, open plain will have no rapids and no whitewater.

In the United States, the volume is measured in cubic feet per second (cfs). This represents how many cubic feet of water flow past any fixed point on the shore during any given second. An average-size creek would likely flow at 100 cfs, while the Mississippi River may well have over 100,000 cfs flowing between its banks in flood.

A river's gradient is measured in feet per mile drop. Gradient is determined by measuring the vertical fall (in feet) of the river, relative to a fixed distance (measured in miles). In other words, gradient measures how steep the hill is that the river is flowing down. Today expert rafters sometimes run rivers with 250 feet per mile gradients. This is considered extremely steep and, until recently, unrunnable. In contrast, the average gradient of the Colorado River is a mere 6 feet per mile. However, the Colorado makes up for what it lacks in gradient by what it has in volume, which is often up to 20,000 cfs. Keep in mind that gradient as a measure of difficulty can be deceiving. For example, an average drop of 50 feet per mile could possibly mean 2 feet per mile with a 48-foot waterfall at the end.

Obstacles refer to all the things that constrict, restrain, squeeze, cramp, arrest, muzzle, block, obstruct, restrict, impede, and otherwise inhibit a river's course from point A to point B.

The Colorado River's Crystal Rapid provides a good example of how volume, gradient, and obstacles interact to create whitewater rapids. The Colorado is a "big volume" river through the Grand Canyon. On a normal day the Glen Canyon Dam releases a peak of over 20,000 cfs of water careening down the majestic mile-deep canyon. After powering air conditioners in Phoenix and before watering lawns in Los Angeles, the river moves slowly through pools, faster through drops. Much of the time, the Colorado River is cool, calm, and collected—nothing more than a beautiful river meandering through spectacular scenery. However, at Crystal Rapid, the river suddenly drops over 17 feet in less than a quarter mile. This 20,000 cfs dropping so quickly didn't make one of the world's biggest rapids all by itself. No, it wasn't until after nearby Crystal Creek flooded, constricting the entire channel with small rocks and putting one BIG one right in the middle, that Crystal became the rafter's nemesis that it is today.

## Obstacles

Obstacles need to be looked at closely—first here and later on the river. Whereas volume and gradient contribute to the danger and power of an obstacle, ultimately it is the obstacle itself that you as a river rafter must overcome, not the river's flow or drop.

The first time you look at a rapid, it will seem to be a maelstrom of white, uncontrolled chaos. Upon further reflection, however, you will find that there are specific, quantifiable parts to that hurricane of aerated river water, which, when mixed together, make up the rapid itself. These parts are the obstacles or problems that you must address, avoid, and ultimately overcome when navigating your raft through the rapid.

## *River Constriction*

When a river narrows and the walls become steeper, you can expect the quality of the rapids to change. In and of itself, river constriction will not produce an obstacle. But in conjunction with steep gradient and high volume, a constricted riverbed can be an obstacle. When a river's walls begin to steepen and the channel begins to tighten, the river is being constricted by geological forces. When this happens, tighten your lifejacket and prepare for a rapid. It may not come, but the conditions are prime. In Deep Throat Rapid on the Zambezi River, a 1-mile-wide section of river funnels through a 10-yard-wide channel. The forced result is a roaring, turbulent, and marginally runnable rapid.

## *Rocks and Boulders*

Rocks epitomize the concept of an obstacle. They are hard, unmoving, and often difficult to avoid. Above water, a house-size boulder can sometimes choke a channel and make passage difficult, if not impossible. Some big rocks have water that flows underneath, making a swim dangerous. Others are sharp and can rip boats. Still others are configured in such a way as to invite the unwary rafter to "wrap" the boat around the rock or flip it upside down. (See Chapter 4 for more information on "wrapping" a boat.)

When submerged, rocks create waves, holes, eddies, and other hydraulic phenomena. Learn to spot rocks. Observe how moving water interacts with rocks. Avoid collisions with rocks. If not, you might give the term "rock and roll" a new meaning. As you become more adept at navigating around rocks, take a moment to look at their beautiful surfaces. They are often sculpted by countless years of flowing waters and seem to hold secrets to a long distant history.

## *Pour-over Rocks*

Pay particular attention to rocks hidden just under the surface of the water. Difficult to see, these "pour-over" rocks have gotten many a rafter stuck in the middle of some very large rapids. If they are sharp, they can ruin your rafting experience in a hurry.

# Waves

Waves are characterized by high peaks and low troughs. Unlike their famous ocean counterparts, river waves stay mostly in one place and are often called "standing waves." Waves come in many sizes, shapes, and strengths. Some break back upon themselves; some are glassy mountains of pure surfing heaven. Some are shaped like a "V"; others are side-curling. Waves have personalities all their own and should be treated with respect—especially when they're bigger than your boat.

A breaking wave is characterized by water falling down the face of a big standing wave. Often mistaken for a hole, breaking waves can eat a boat alive. If the amount of water falling down the face of the wave is substantial, running into a breaking wave can be like hitting a wall. Big and white, a breaking wave (Figure 3-3) is usually easily seen and avoided—or seen and attempted.

A V-wave is formed by river constriction, steep gradient, and big volume. Its name describes it perfectly. If you were to look down on

## Figure 3-3

**A raft hitting a wave**

top of a V-wave it would look like a "V," with the bottom of the "V" facing downstream. From a rafter's perspective, V-waves can be tricky and are the cause of many a flipped boat.

A side-curling wave resembles one half of the V-wave. Sometimes breaking, sometimes not, a side-curling wave is best characterized by the angle at which it is met by the current. Unlike a wave that you meet head-on, a side-curler comes from the side. For this reason you have to keep an eye out for it because it can flip your boat.

The perfect surfing wave is a tall, steep wall of glass. Not breaking back, not side-curling, the perfect surfing wave is revered the world over. You will often see kayakers glued to the face of these waves, not moving upstream or downstream, but caught in perfect balance. It is even possible to surf a raft on such a wave, but techniques have yet to be perfected.

## Holes

Holes are characterized by a vortex of powerful contradictory surface currents. Much like their celestial brethren, black holes, once you end up in a river hole, it often feels as if you might have to pass through the fourth dimension to get out of it.

A hole is created when the river falls quickly over an obstacle. The resulting low pressure zone downstream of the obstacle is filled in with surface water that actually flows back upstream. The place where the downstream current meets the upstream current is the hole, and floating items (such as boats, people, paddles, and coolers) can easily get stuck there. You can expect quite a ride while stuck in a hole, hence the terms "washing machined" and "recycled" to describe this experience. Learn to spot holes and take care: The holes that appear most calm are often the most hazardous.

## Dams, Ledges, Pylons, and Bridges

Beware of anything man-made in a river. Besides being an aesthetic abomination, man-made structures such as low-head dams, ledges, pylons, and bridges are usually dangerous and should be avoided. Low-head dams are particularly dangerous because the holes created at their bases are perfectly formed and almost impossible to escape. The strange part is that the hole formed at the bottom of a dam looks very calm. There isn't a lot of whitewater. But don't let this fool you.

*Figure 3-4*

### Surface current flowing upstream

*All* the surface current is flowing back upstream into the hole (Figure 3-4).

This same kind of perfectly formed hole can sometimes be caused by a natural formation such as a ledge. A major clue indicating the possible presence of a hole is surface current flowing back upstream.

## Trees

Trees and their limbs are a hazard and should be avoided. Unlike other obstacles, trees create "strainers" that can ensnare floating things such as rafts and swimmers. Trees can strain the unwary rafter in much the same manner that a colander strains spaghetti. It is not a pretty sight nor a laughing matter when a swimmer becomes plastered up against a tree limb, pinned there by the force of literally tons of water. To prevent this, the best rule is to avoid any and all trees that are in the river.

## Waterfalls

Waterfalls are caused when a river suddenly flows over a vertical or nearly vertical drop. They range in size from 1 foot to 1,000 feet, and where the falling water meets the bottom, there is almost inevitably a hole. Often this is a very powerful hole. Waterfalls that drop more than a couple of feet are not the domain of rafts and should be approached cautiously and, if possible, avoided.

## Eddies—Usually a Rafter's Best Friend

No one is sure where the term "eddy" came from. Many wild stories come to mind—none of them true. Eddies are found behind rocks and next to riverbanks. An important feature of every rapid, eddies are often the most difficult feature to see. Eddies are formed by the same process that forms holes. A zone of low pressure is created behind the obstacle, which is then filled in with water from behind. This means that the water in an eddy flows upstream.

As one might imagine, the place where the eddy's upstream current meets the downstream current can produce some turbulence. This point of agitation is called an "eddy line" and can create an obstacle in itself. It is important to learn to recognize eddies because, as we will learn later in Chapter 5, they are a key component in rafting technique.

Whitewater results when rivers flow rapidly through, over, and around a mixture of waves, holes, rocks, eddies, swirls, and waterfalls. It roars, bucks, and, strangely enough, often beckons. With proper knowledge, equipment, training, and respect, you can experience its moods and appreciate its freedoms.

# SAFETY FIRST

R iver running is safe. Professional guides often say, "The most dangerous part of a river trip is driving to the put-in." With proper knowledge and preparation, this is true. This book covers only the essentials of rafting and should not be used without proper on-river training. Take it with you on training expeditions with qualified guides. Get it wet. The truth is that this book can give you the basics, but nothing beats hands-on training.

This chapter will focus on the major safety issues to keep in mind before you get on the river. It begins with a brief discussion on whitewater schools, followed by tips on assessing a river's difficulty, first-aid training, and the put-in talk.

Probably the most basic safety point to remember is to take your time. People learn at different paces, so don't be pressured into going on a river or through a rapid that you don't feel comfortable with. In Russia, where rafting is done by organized clubs, it often takes many years of dedicated rafting for a member to develop the skills necessary to run difficult rivers. In contrast, many less experienced commercial clients in the United States have the opportunity to run difficult rivers, led by skilled guides who know rivers and their potential hazards. As you begin to explore the thrills of whitewater rafting, go slow. Take your time. Simply experiencing the river's magic is special.

# Whitewater Schools: Become a Doctor of "Rivertology"

Rafting a whitewater river takes experience and knowledge. This book will provide you with some basic knowledge, but no matter how hard you try, or how sophisticated book printing technology becomes, it just isn't going to get you wet. That's up to you. In order to safely gain the experience you need, you must find a teacher.

There is no better way to find a teacher than to go to school—whitewater school, that is. Whitewater schools with the expressed intent of teaching the student to safely raft on whitewater rivers are run by professional outfitters, college-affiliated outdoor education programs, and whitewater clubs. A good whitewater school will allow you to take the principles from this book and put them into practice. There is simply no better, safer, more time-efficient way to gain the experience you need to make proper decisions on the river.

Whitewater schools range in length from one-day seminars to two-week extravaganzas on several rivers. In the United States, schools are conducted mostly in the spring. There are many good schools out there. Some criteria with which to judge whether the whitewater school you are considering is a good one are:

•The reputation and safety record of the company or organization offering the whitewater school. How long has it offered whitewater schools?

•Does it offer written material with its training?

•Does it offer mini-seminars? What are the topics?

•What are the skill levels of the teachers? What are their qualifications? What is the ratio of teachers to students? (1:5 is good.)

•Does the school allow you to raft on many different kinds of rivers and learn in many different kinds of boats?

Choosing a whitewater school is very important because, in addition to learning the skills of rafting, you will be learning a rafting style. It is also important to select a whitewater school that meshes well with your personality—especially if you're interested in becoming a commercial guide or working for a club. Many organizations use whitewater schools as training grounds for their next season's guides, and there is no better way of getting your foot in the door (or paddle in the water, as the case may be) than by participating fully in that organization's whitewater school. Do some research, make some calls, and find out if the people offering the whitewater school meet your standards of excellence.

## Classifying the River's Difficulty

Rivers are classified in many different ways. In the Midwest, rivers are rated on a 1–10 scale ranging from easiest to most difficult. In Europe and Russia there are different variants. However, over the years an international standard has emerged. This internationally recognized rating system has six levels of difficulty: Class I–VI. Nowadays, the only remaining point of contention among river runners lies with Class VI and its status as a runnable rapid. Some say that Class VI defines unrunnable; others say that it is the outer limit of runnable. The following rating system definitions include both Class VI points of view:

*Class I*: Moving water with small waves. Few or no obstructions.

*Class II*: Easy rapids with waves up to 3 feet high and with wide, clear channels that are obvious without scouting. Some maneuvering required.

*Class III*: Rapids with high, irregular waves often capable of capsizing a boat. Narrow passages that may require complex maneuvering. May require scouting from shore.

*Class IV:* Long, difficult rapids with constricted passages that often require precise maneuvering in very turbulent waters. Scouting from shore is often necessary, and conditions make rescue difficult.

*Class V:* Extremely difficult, long, and very violent rapids with highly congested routes that nearly always must be scouted from shore. Rescue conditions are difficult, and there is significant hazard to life in the event of a mishap.

*Class VI:* Nearly impossible and very dangerous. May be runnable by a top team of experts, but not recommended.

## Assessing the River Classification System

When someone advises you that a river is an "easy Class III" or a "gnarly Class V," my advice is to take this information with a grain of salt. River and weather conditions can change quickly and significantly affect a river's difficulty. For example, a Class III stream can be transformed into a raging Class V monster after a warm rain in spring. *Therefore, the river rating system described above should be used as a guide only, not as an absolute measure of a river's difficulty.*

When judging the difficulty of a river, keep in mind the three factors of volume, gradient, and obstacles discussed in Chapter 3. Is there a lot of water in the river (high volume)? More than normal? How many feet per mile does the river drop (what is the gradient)? Are there recovery pools between the rapids or continuous, nonstop whitewater? Does the river flow through a narrow, constricted gorge or an open, meandering valley? What is the geology of the area? This information used in conjunction with the river rating system, an accurate weather forecast, the water temperature, and difficulty of evacuation can help you to assess the river. As river professional Mike Grant says, the best motto to follow when you're getting yourself ready for a river trip is: "Pack light and be prepared for anything."

# The Team

A key element to any safe, fun rafting trip is the experience level of the team. Ascertaining the health and experience of each member is important. If a problem should occur far from a road or immediate help, you need to know whom you're dealing with and how much you can count on your teammates. Generally, the more difficult the river, the more experience and higher level of fitness you and your team should possess.

If you're going rafting as a client on a commercial trip, assess the river's difficulty by using this guide, judge your skill and health, and go with a licensed outfitter with a proven safety record.

# First-Aid Basics

Knowledge of first-aid basics is important. I recommend that you take a Red Cross Basic First-Aid and CPR class if you are serious about learning to raft. *Basic Essentials: First Aid* is also very informative. Almost all commercial outfitters in the United States require that their guides know CPR and basic first aid, while many companies require an even higher standard of first-aid certification. In the pages that follow, I have chosen to focus several specific, river-related first-aid issues. This section is not intended to be a substitute for a first-aid class, but it will provide you with some of the essentials of rafting first aid.

## *Hypothermia*

Hypothermia, commonly called exposure, is caused when the core body temperature drops below its normal level. This can occur after a swim in cold water or even while paddling on a chilly day. The early symptoms of hypothermia are exhaustion, shaking, and loss of coordination, which can lead to slurred speech and a semi-comatose state. Contrary to popular belief, extremely cold weather is not required for hypothermia. In fact, most deaths attributed to hypothermia occur at relatively warm temperatures (between 40 and 50 degrees Fahrenheit).

Hypothermia can be very dangerous and should be taken seriously. Watch for this condition at all times on a river trip, particularly if the water is cold and/or the weather is poor. Prevention is the best way to deal with hypothermia. Wear appropriate warm clothes in camp and wet or dry suits while on the water.

In the event that anyone develops the symptoms of hypothermia, stop. Then slowly warm the victim. This means get to shore if you're out on the river. Light a fire, get the victim into warm, dry clothes, and put the victim in a sleeping bag with other warm bodies. Give the victim a warm, nonalcoholic drink. These warming techniques should only be used if the victim is conscious. If the victim is unconscious, this indicates a more advanced stage of hypothermia. In this case, "riverside" warming techniques will not be sufficient treatment; the victim must be evacuated to a hospital immediately.

## Drowning

Drowning is suffocation. When a person is submerged under water and unable to breathe, drowning may result. Water need not be inhaled directly into the lungs. Without a constant flow of oxygen, the brain can only last a few minutes without damage. Where there is water, there is the possibility of drowning. This is why lifejackets must be worn and why safe procedures must be followed—at all times—when rafting.

## Cardiopulmonary Resuscitation

Cardiopulmonary resuscitation, or CPR, refers to a practice you can learn that saves lives. CPR is used when a victim's heart has stopped and/or when a victim is not breathing. Given that the potential of drowning exists when river running, and that you may often be far away from immediate medical assistance, it is important for you to know how to administer CPR. Classes are taught by local hospitals and the Red Cross. Call for details. The only way to learn CPR is to take a class—it cannot be learned on your own.

# Safety Equipment

In order to have a safe, enjoyable river trip, you must always wear the following equipment. Lifejackets, manufactured to U.S. Coast Guard–approved standards, are a must and should be worn at all times by every person. A well-designed lifejacket will be comfortable to wear and will protect you by bringing you to the surface if you fall in. Don't be deceived by seemingly calm water; keep your lifejacket on!

Helmets are a good idea in all rafting. In the United States many commercial companies only require them on the more difficult runs, but in Europe everyone wears them all the time. Helmets will protect you not only from rocks but also from other hard objects like oars, paddles, frames, and other people's heads.

Wet and dry suits are important safety items when the water is

# PLAYING IT SAFE—CARRY THE RIGHT GEAR

River running is enjoyable and safe when certain precautions are taken. Whether you're a river guide or passenger, you should be prepared on every trip by wearing or having:

- **A U.S. Coast Guard–approved lifejacket**—sometimes called a PFD, or personal flotation device. Today there are many PFDs that are made specifically for the rigors of whitewater boating. As a commercial passenger, you will likely be provided a lifejacket. Make sure it's snug yet comfortable and doesn't ride up over your head when someone tugs on the shoulder straps.

- **A wet or dry suit.** The purpose of a wet or dry suit isn't so much to keep you dry as it is to keep you warm. When choosing your river clothing, you should dress prepared to swim down the longest rapid on the river and not get cold. Depending on how cold conditions may be, there are a number of dressing combinations available ranging from full body wet suits, to dry suits lined with full body pile, to windbreaking paddle jackets, to light Neoprene vests. Check with your local outfitter to find out what is needed on any particular river; they may or may not provide this sort of gear.

- **A helmet.** There are a number of great whitewater helmets on the market. All helmets should cover the entire head, temples, and ears. They should be snug yet comfortable. Most outfitters will provide helmets, but check to be sure.

- **A throw bag.** Every raft should have this simple bag of rope that is designed to snag swimmers from the water.

- **A first-aid kit.** The length and difficulty of the river and the distance or difficulty of a potential evacuation will dictate the need for either a simple first-aid setup, or an expedition-level first-aid kit.

- **A repair kit.** Better have one of these, which includes glue, material, and odds and ends to keep the raft afloat in the event of a popped tube, bent frame, or broken oarlock. The kit should be checked before each trip. It is rather disheartening to rip the tube of your beautiful raft, open your repair kit, and discover glue that has long ago turned to rock or has exploded and oozed all over the material. (I've had both of these experiences on rivers in Africa and Russia . . . let me tell you, it isn't fun.)

cold. The bottom line is that they will keep you warm. Neoprene wet suits made fashionable by surfers throughout the world keep you warm by trapping a layer of insulated water next to your skin. Dry suits work by keeping the water out altogether. Either a wet or dry suit must be worn when hypothermia conditions are possible.

## The Put-in Talk

An important element of a safe journey down the river is making sure that everyone understands certain safety and emergency procedures. The put-in talk should cover what to do if a problem arises and, just as important, how to avoid potentially dangerous situations in the first place. The put-in talk should review the safety practices to follow while on the river. This talk is usually given by the leader at the beginning of every trip and starts something like this: "I know everybody is eager to get on the water, but I want to have everyone's undivided attention for the next fifteen minutes. It is very important that everyone understands what I am about to say. . . ." Put-in talk points to remember include:

• Avoid entanglement: Keep all rigging and other lines coiled.

• Never tie or otherwise "attach" yourself to a boat. You can imagine how dangerous this would be if your boat flipped.

• Wear foot protection.

• Keep your lifejacket securely fastened at all times.

• The best way to avoid an emergency is by becoming the best possible team. Work hard, but stay alert and calm.

Put-in talks will focus on the following points: swims, wraps, flips, holes, and land dangers.

### Swims

The most likely problem that will occur on a river trip is that somewhere in a rapid someone will fall out of the raft into the river. While this is usually not serious, everyone on the trip must fully understand what to do in this situation. If you fall in the river, the first things that you'll notice are that it's cold, dark, and wet and that you can't breathe. This often leads to a natural response known as PANIC! However, if you can remember only one point from the put-in talk, remember not to panic if you fall in the water. You will come to the surface almost immediately—thanks to your securely fastened lifejacket. Then, if at all possible, relax and enjoy the ride.

Keep in mind that, ultimately, it is your responsibility to get yourself out of the river. The more difficult and dangerous the river, the more this is true.

Some other important points to remember if you fall in the water:
•If you come up under a boat, move hand over hand to the side of the boat.

•If you can, get back in the boat immediately. Ask for help from someone still in the boat.

•If you cannot get immediately back in the boat, move into a seated position with legs pointed downstream, knees slightly bent, and toes held high (Figure 4-1). This is very important to remember, since this position will help to protect you if you collide with a rock or other obstacles in the river.

•Avoid getting between the path of a boat and a rock.

•Do not try to stand up in swift moving, shallow water. By standing, you make it possible for your legs to be wedged in the rocks and your body to be pinned underwater.

**Direction of Current**

*Figure 4-1*

**Correct swimming position**

***Rafting***

31

- Stay far away from trees in the river. They create "strainers" that can trap and drag a swimmer underwater.

- Get out on shore or into another boat as soon as possible.

- The rest of the team should remain calm and not jump into the river to save a swimmer.

## Wraps

Wraps are caused when a raft hits an exposed rock sideways. If emergency procedures are not followed quickly, the boat may become pasted flat around the upstream face of the rock. This happens when the boat is being pushed downstream by the current, but the rock stops its progress. If the raft does not slide around the rock, the current can actually push the upstream tube under the water, raising the downstream tube and wrapping the boat tight around the rock (Figure 4-2). You can avoid a wrap if everyone in the boat moves to the rock side immediately upon contact. Wraps can take hours and sometimes days to get the boat off the rock, so you definitely want to avoid them whenever possible.

On the Rangataiki River in New Zealand, a very steep continuous,

*Figure 4-2*

**A wrap**

## RIVER HARDWARE

River hardware, that funny stuff guides have on their lifejackets, serves some critically important safety purposes:

• **The river knife**—a razor-sharp, quickly available tool that never sees a block of cheese or a can of tuna. The river knife is used during any emergency that might require the immediate cutting of a line or raft tube.

• **Carabiners**—an oval clip developed for rock climbing. The carabiner is used to clip gear and water bottles to the raft and to set up a Z-pulley system to free a wedged or wrapped raft.

• **Pulleys**—developed originally for rock climbing, pulleys are kept available to set up a Z-pulley system.

• **Webbing belt**—a piece of ¾-1 inch webbing wrapped three times and worn around the waist. The buckle is usually a carabiner. This is used to clip onto the D-ring of an overturned raft while floating down the river to gain leverage to right the boat.

• **A whistle**—a must-have item for the river professional. The whistle allows communication between guides over the often deafening roar of the rapids.

rocky river in the North Island, one of our guides on a commercial trip wrapped a boat in the middle of a long rapid. We spend the first two hours getting the cold and dejected crew safely off the wrapped boat. By the time we got them to shore, it was beginning to get dark. The guides decided to leave the wrapped raft overnight and pick it up the next day. We returned the next afternoon and tried for three hours to pull the boat off the rock. It was getting late again, and all the commercial clients were growing restless. So, in desperation, we decided to cut the floor out in order to let the water flow through.

I moved out to the raft on a rope, with the intention of cutting a small hole in the floor to release some of the tension that trapped the raft against the rock. The result when I touched the floor with the blade was swift. The raft's floor was immediately shredded, and the boat exploded into the air as the pressure of the tons of water that had been holding it to the rock was released. It had taken six hours over a

*Rafting*

period of two days and an entire floor to get this boat off the rock.

Some important points to remember if your raft hits a rock:

• Move quickly to the side of the raft that has hit the rock.

• Do this when your guide yells, "Rock Slide!" This takes weight off the upstream tube and can prevent a wrap.

• Avoid getting between a raft and a rock if you fall in the water.

• If your raft becomes wrapped around a rock, set up a Z-pulley system to drag it off the rock (Figure 4-3).

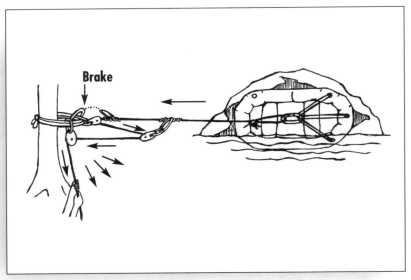

*Figure 4-3*

**Z-pulley system**

*Flips*

Regarding flipping rafts upside down (Figures 4-4 and 4-5) in a big rapid, there is a saying in the business: "There are those who have flipped, and those who are going to." Eventually somewhere, sometime, your boat will hit a wave, drop into a hole, or careen off a rock, and before you know it, up and over the raft will go. The first thing to keep in mind is that all the rules for swimming rapids apply.

The only big difference is that instead of one swimmer, there is a whole boatload!

There is a rapid on the Klamath River in California called "Big Ike." In the spring of 1983 the Klamath was flooding and I had been guiding commercial clients through the rapid on a regular basis. A huge breaking wave pulses in the middle of Big Ike. It was avoidable, but my crew and I were having such a good day that we were feeling adventurous. "I reckon we have a 50-50 chance of staying upright in this one," I informed my crew. After their enthusiastic encouragement, we went straight into the middle of Big Ike. The flip was instantaneous, the power awesome. The force of the water alone was enough to blow a patch off the boat, bend a frame of solid steel tubing, and rip three lashed dry bags off the stern. It was a humbling experience.

## Figure 4-4

**A paddle boat flip on the Zambezi River**

## Figure 4-5

**Bottoms up!**

Some important points to remember if your raft flips:

• If you come up underneath your raft, take a breath and then move hand over hand to the side.

• Unless there is a serious hazard downstream, stay with your raft on the upstream side. If there is a hazard, swim away from the boat.

• Try to climb on top of your overturned raft.

• Look for help from another boat. Try to paddle or swim your overturned raft to shore.

## *Holes*

It is possible to get a raft stuck in a hole. It is also possible to become stuck in a hole while you're swimming. In either case, relax and try to think clearly. I was caught in a huge hole in rapid #18 on the Zambezi River in Africa for a full sixty seconds. Now, that may not seem like a long time in the "real" world, but in the white, wild, rodeo-like world of holes, ten seconds seems like an eternity. All I could think about was moving to the downstream side of the boat—the side of the boat that was going to go high. One of the passengers held tight to the bow line and the video shows her doing a perfect end-over-end flip out of the raft. She received high marks and cheers for her pointed toes from all the judges sitting on the rocks. The boat was eventually ejected from the hole—upright this time.

Some important points to remember if your raft gets stuck in a hole:

• Move quickly to the downstream side of the boat.

• The raft may rotate, so keep moving to the downstream side of the boat.

• If possible, use your paddle to pull your raft out of the hole.

• If you get stuck in a hole when swimming, relax. Be ready to take a breath whenever your lifejacket brings your head above water. You may find yourself being "washing-machined," or caught in a cycle of being repeatedly pulled underwater, then pushed above water. Don't panic. Within a few seconds, you most likely will be propelled out of the hole. If you continue to recirculate back into the hole, try to move to one side of the hole. Don't fight the current.

## The Real Danger—Land

Although I emphasize safe river practices, the fact is that most river trip accidents occur on land: scouting rapids, in camp, portaging the boats, chopping firewood. The best motto: *Watch your step*. Rocks are slippery. Plants may cause rashes. Insects sting. Campfires are hot. Stay alert.

# Ecological Practices

We share rivers with many other people and species. Not many pristine rivers still exist today, so it is vital that we do not contribute to polluting rivers or their banks. In fact, we should try to leave the rivers that we explore cleaner than when we arrived. Then our children's children can enjoy these wonderful places, too.

Some ecological points to remember:

• Never litter. Cigarette butts, food scraps, and plastic wrappers are litter.

• Unless instructed to do so, never wash your body or dishes with soap directly in the river.

• Pick up trash along the way.

• Don't use the river as a substitute for a toilet.

• Carry appropriate sanitation facilities with you.

• Take only photographs; leave only footprints.

# Scouting and Portaging

Whenever you come to a rapid where you can't see the bottom, or you can't see a clear path through it, STOP. It's time to scout. Scouting means pulling over to the side of the river, walking down the bank to assess the difficulty of the rapid, and planning the best way through or around it. This is the time when most river runners get butterflies in their stomachs. Generally rapids that necessitate a scout are either long, difficult, steep, dangerous, or all of these things.

Portaging (Figure 4-6), or walking around a rapid, is what separates the shrewd river runner from the foolish one. When confronted with a rapid that is beyond his or her capabilities, the shrewd river runner will opt to portage. The foolish river runner, in contrast, will often be

## Figure 4-6

**Carrying rafts can be done by rolling the raft lengthwise into the form of a snake**

swayed into running an unsafe rapid by peer pressure, undue *machismo*, sheer ignorance, or all three. This is stupid. There is always another challenging rapid around the bend, and it's not worth risking injury or worse. Know your abilities. Also, realize that running rapids is a very psychologically demanding activity and your abilities can change from day to day, even hour to hour.

Once, when exploring the North Fork of the Mokulomne River in California, our team came upon a very steep rapid. As we pulled our raft over to the bank to scout, one of the kayakers who had already scouted the rapid met us at shore looking very dejected. "The rapid is unrunnable and unportageable," he said, staring bleakly ahead. He was right about it being unportageable—the sheer granite walls extended vertically on either side of the canyon for many thousands of feet. Luckily, however, he was mistaken about its runnability. After the most tense scout I have ever experienced, which lasted well over two hours, we successfully ran the rapid.

## Don't Boat Alone

A good rule is to always go rafting with at least one other boat. In the event that something happens, such as an injury or a ripped raft, you are not alone.

These guidelines give you an idea of how to avoid problems and what to do if they occur. Bill McGinnis, a mentor of mine who is an expert river runner and commercial outfitter, teaches a very valuable lesson to all of his guides: If a crisis situation occurs on a river trip, do not ask yourself, Who did wrong? Or, How did I get here? Rather ask yourself, Where am I? And, How do I get to where I want to go? It is often easy to look for scapegoats when a situation becomes tense. However, on the river, especially in a crisis situation, there is little time to place blame. When a crisis occurs, it is time for thoughtful and appropriate action. Probably the best guiding philosophy on the river, as in life, is to use your best judgment. Learn as much as you can and practice, practice, practice.

# READ AND RUN

T he art and beauty of river running comes from a guide's ability to "read" the rapids' mood and difficulty and then "run" the raft successfully through the rapid. This section focuses on the process of reading and safely running the rapids.

## Reading the River

Look downstream, figure out what is down there, determine what is safe, and decide where to go. River guides call this "reading" the rapid. And, like reading a good book, reading a challenging rapid is often open to a certain amount of interpretation. What's the main plot? Where am I going? Who are the characters? Where should I focus my attention? Some folks focus on waves, others on holes, and yet others on the entrance to the rapid or on the recovery pool at the bottom.

It is important to observe the rapid in its entirety as much as possible. When scouting Crystal Rapid (one of the biggest rapids on the Colorado River through the Grand Canyon) for the first time, I became so entranced by the famous Crystal hole that I neglected to study the waves at the entrance to the rapid. Because of this, I ended up headfirst in the middle of Crystal's monstrous hole. Needless to say, I lived and I learned that it is critical to study all parts of a rapid before plunging headfirst into it. The best river readers absorb the rapid completely, intuiting difficulties and dangers from past experience while at the same time planning the best, safest, and most exciting routes through the maelstrom.

Reading a rapid is as much an art as a science. It requires a new way of looking. A key step is identifying the downstream obstacles. Are there standing waves or a big hole ahead? Is the eddy behind that rock strong enough to hold the boat? Is that a wave or a pour-over rock? The next step is deciding where to go—choosing your route around, over, and through the obstacles. Finally, you must execute your decision and get the boat to go where you want to go. I call this entire process the RIDE.

# RIDE: Read, Identify, Decide, Execute

*Read*. Reading means looking downstream and observing the river and the movement of its waters. It is the least tangible and most important step in the RIDE process. It requires the type of attentive observation used by a race car driver on a winding road, a downhill skier in moguls, or a tennis player in a challenging volley. The best way to develop the skill of reading rapids is to practice. I find it helps to watch other people navigate a rapid, or go to your nearest creek and float a stick or leaf. Watch how the current affects the floating objects.

*Identify*. The second important step in successfully reading a rapid is to identify specific obstacles. Where are the holes, waves, rocks? Which of these are safe to run? Which must I avoid? Where is the current likely to take me? Is it where I want to go? Identifying obstacles can be very difficult, especially from water level. This takes time and practice, and is absolutely necessary for a successful RIDE.

Sometimes when the rapid is very steep, you have little time to read the rapid and to identify its obstacles. That is why watching other boats or simply taking the time to point out obstacles to yourself from the calm of the shore will teach you to read and identify quickly and instinctively on the river, in the middle of a rapid.

*Decide*. The third step in the RIDE process is to decide. Where do I go and how do I get there? By combining the information you gained by reading and identifying with your knowledge of the raft's abilities to maneuver (which we will learn more about in the next chapter), you can then decide on the course of action.

Reading the rapid, identifying the obstacles, and deciding on the course of action is a process that happens quickly and many times in the course of running a single rapid. It is a dynamic process in which you constantly assimilate changing information and decide where to go and what to avoid. At first, while you are learning, it is valuable to break down the basic steps of the RIDE process until they become second nature.

*Execute.* Finally, after reading the river, identifying the obstacles, and deciding on the course of action, it is time to execute—to act on your decision and *put the boat in the current that is going where you want to go.* This final step in the RIDE process is the crux to learning how to guide a raft successfully through the rapids.

Generally, currents in a rapid are strong. The bigger the rapid, the stronger the currents. Trying to fight them or move against them is, for the most part, futile. You must learn how to use the force of the water to your advantage. That is why the final component of RIDE, execute, is so important. In executing your plan of action, you put the raft in the current that is going where you want to go. Bill McGinnis stresses this concept over and over in his whitewater school in California. But you are only able to put the boat in the current that is going where you want to go after you *know* where you want to go. That is why the entire RIDE process of reading, identifying, deciding, and executing is so important.

The RIDE process has been successfully used by river rafters everywhere—from Russian catamaran masters challenging the frigid waters of Siberia, to Grand Canyon river rats in their mighty thirty-passenger "J" rigs, to world-champion slalom raft racers. As you gain more rafting experience, the RIDE process will become second nature to you, as well. It's only a matter of practice.

## Ferry Angles

A ferry angle is the angle at which a raft is rowed or paddled relative to the current. You will use ferry angles when your boat is in a current that is moving toward an obstacle you want to avoid. Speeding up or slowing down the boat will not suffice. The only way to avoid the obstacle is to turn the boat *at an angle to the current* and row or paddle away. To *where,* you ask? Toward *the current that's going where you want to go,* of course.

Picture your paddle raft floating down the river. While reading the river, you identify an obstacle ahead. A big rock lies directly in your path. The current you are in flows directly into that rock. You decide to *put the boat in the current that is going where you want to go* and look around. Where is that current? Downstream the clearest channel is to the left of the big rock. The current moving to that channel is also to your left about 20 feet away. You turn the boat to the left, and move toward that current. The angle of the raft relative to the current you have just chosen, the ferry angle, is the key to any successful whitewater maneuvering (Figure 5-1).

## Upstream Ferry Angles

Ferry angles are divided into two types: upstream and downstream. Upstream angles are used when the raft moves upstream relative to the current. The result of a properly executed upstream ferry angle (Figure 5-2) is that the boat moves laterally from side to side without moving downstream.

For example, ferry boats that take people and vehicles from one side of the river to the other and back without moving downstream use upstream ferry angles exclusively. These ferries do this by pointing their bow almost directly upstream, with a slight angle toward their destination. Upstream angles are often used by oar boat guides, as they row upstream against the current, to put the raft in the current that is going where they want to go.

*Figure 5-1*

**Whitewater maneuvering**

*Figure 5-2*

**Upstream ferry angle**

### *Downstream Ferry Angles*

Downstream ferry angles are used more by paddle boats. Unlike upstream ferry angles, which slow or actually eliminate a raft's downstream progression, downstream ferry angles use the force of the current to propel a boat both downstream and side to side across the current. An aggressive maneuver, the downstream angle (Figure 5-3) is used often in swift, big whitewater.

## Momentum

Momentum refers to the measure of a raft's motion, equal to the product of its mass and speed in the river. A heavy paddle raft being propelled will have a great deal of momentum. In contrast, a light oar boat using an upstream ferry angle to get away from a rock will have very little momentum.

Momentum is an important concept in river rafting because it helps get your raft through holes, around rocks, and over waves. Without momentum, waves can stop and sometimes flip a boat. With

*Figure 5-3*

**Downstream ferry angle**

it, you can sometimes power over the same waves. Any time you move the raft with your paddles or oars you build up momentum.

In large-volume rivers where the size of the waves can very well dwarf your raft, momentum is critical in keeping your boat upright. For example, a raft trying to go over a big river wave has two conflicting forces exerted upon it. On the one hand, the raft is being pushed downstream by the force of the current. On the other, as the boat begins to climb up the face of the wave, a new, powerful force comes into play—gravity. Unless sufficient momentum is generated by the current and your paddle strokes to carry your boat up and over the wave, gravity might prove the superior force and flip your raft upside down (Figure 5-4).

In Hance Rapid in the Grand Canyon, there are three big waves on the far right side at the bottom of the rapid. Prudent rafters avoid them, but I decided to take a small, light 12-foot oar boat through the waves. It was youthful folly to be sure, but I didn't have any crew members who could potentially fall overboard and the waves didn't look *that* big. The first wave was fun. The second stopped my

*Figure 5-4*

**Failure to gain momentum can result in a flipped raft**

downstream momentum. As I rose up the face of the final wave, I felt the raft slow down. Although the current was racing downstream, suddenly my raft slid backwards down the face of the wave. The wave caught the raft's right tube and threw it high into the air. A precarious balance, then gravity prevailed; I flipped and learned a powerful lesson about momentum.

Momentum also plays a critical role when going through big holes. Like big waves, holes have two powerful conflicting forces that work on a raft—a downstream current and a surface current moving upstream. Unless you build up enough momentum to counteract the forces of the upstream surface current, that upstream surface current can stop your forward momentum and take you backwards into the hole. There you meet the powerful downstream current, and the result is a wild ride and, very possibly, a flip.

## Straight Ahead

The bigger, nastier, and uglier the wave or hole you are about to enter, the more important it is that you hit it straight on. A raft that strays sideways into a big wave or hole (Figure 5-5) is headed for trouble. This is because a raft that has lost momentum and is sideways to the current has more surface area for the strong downstream current to grab. It is very rare that you will see a raft slip end over end. A flip almost always occurs when the raft has turned sideways to the current and has lost downstream momentum. Therefore, the point to remember is to keep your raft straight relative to the waves and holes when going through big rapids.

*Figure 5-5*

**A raft going sideways into a hole**

# High-siding

There is a big difference between trying to keep your raft straight with plenty of forward momentum and actually doing it. The fact is, you will often be turned sideways and lose your momentum. When this happens, you high-side. The maneuver is simple: Quickly move to the downstream side of your boat and put your weight on the tube that will soon be forced high into the air.

On the Zambezi River in Africa, the waves and the holes are so big

*Figure 5-6*

**Aggressive high-siding is the key to rafting on the Zambezi River**

that the local rafting companies employ professional "high-siders." These young African "high-siders" travel down the river in commercial rafts with clients, throw themselves from side to side, and do everything possible to keep the rafts upright. A good high-side can make all the difference when a raft is being tossed around like a leaf on a blustery autumn day. High-siding (Figure 5-6) is a skill that you will definitely want to learn—because you are sure to need it out there on the river!

## Using Eddies

Eddies can either help or hinder the rafter. Recognized and used correctly, eddies allow the rafter time to rest and look downstream. They also offer the opportunity for a quick pivot turn. Unrecognized, eddies seem to reach out and spin the raft at the worst possible moment.

To stop in an eddy you must identify it, set a ferry angle toward it, then build up momentum to cross the eddy line. It is important to practice getting smoothly and consistently in and out of eddies, because there will come a time when missing an important eddy might mean an unintentional ride down a rapid that should have been scouted first or perhaps not run at all. Proficient Class V rafters often "eddy hop" their way down continuous steep sections or river, going from eddy to eddy to make their way safely downstream. Catching eddies should be practiced over and over again. It is a very important, basic essential.

Eddies can also be used to slow the raft and to assist in turns. Any part of the raft that goes into an eddy is going to move slower than the part of the raft that is out in the current. When you put only the bow of the boat in an eddy, the stern will quickly pivot around, turning the boat. If you are unprepared for this eddy turn, it can take you off course from where you want to go. If you anticipate and plan for an eddy turn, you can actually use it to your advantage as you further refine the RIDE process.

In this chapter we have explored the basics of reading and running the river. In Chapter 6, we will learn the specific techniques of guiding the raft through the rapid.

# RAFT TECHNIQUE

N ow that we know about different whitewater rafts, understand the elements of a whitewater rapid, are familiar with basic safety essentials, and have learned certain river guiding fundamentals, it is time to learn how to move a boat around.

## Paddle Boat Technique: The Art of Team

No doubt about it, paddle rafting is a team sport. In order to maximize safety *and* fun, the focus is on teamwork: Everybody works together to reach a common goal. Even though people sometimes think, "Ah, it's my vacation and I'll paddle whenever I want," the truth is that one of the most wonderful, exhilarating feelings comes when you and your team work well together. Everyone paddles, and you miss the holes and avoid the big wrap rocks. Best of all, everyone shares the victory of making it through the rapids. Teamwork is one of the key elements of a successful river journey.

Behind every good team is a coach. While this cliché is often used figuratively, it can be applied literally to rafting because in most situations the guide sits in the rear of the boat. Like a good coach, a paddle guide teaches the techniques, calls the plays, and, along with the team, practices, practices, practices.

### *Paddle Boat Commands*

A guide communicates to the team by using a set of predetermined verbal commands. There are five basic commands that a guide uses in a paddle boat: "Forward paddle, back paddle, right turn, left turn," and just as important as the rest, "Stop." The guide should speak loudly and clearly so that these commands can be heard above the rapid's din.

The guide reads the river, identifies the obstacles, decides the course of action, and executes the course by shouting out a command. The team hears the command and responds by performing the correct stroke. This means that team members quickly put their paddles in the water at the same time and make the boat move—either forward, backward, to the right, or to the left.

It is important for team members to synchronize their paddle strokes to obtain the maximum power from their effort. The best way I've found to teach a team to paddle together is by designating one of the forward bow paddlers as the "pacesetter." This person's job is to paddle with a solid, regular rhythm. The other bow person should then stroke in sync with the pacesetter. Then everyone else in the raft can simply copy the strokes of the person in front of them. With a little practice, this is a simple way to ensure that everyone in the raft paddles in sync.

### THE FORWARD STROKE

A "forward!" command is given to tell everyone in the boat to make a forward stroke (Figure 6-1) together. This moves the raft toward the place that the guide wants to go. To make a forward stroke, grip the

**Direction of Raft**

*Figure 6-1*

**Forward stroke**

paddle with one hand at the top and the other midway down the shaft. Then, using your entire body, lean forward, reach out into the water with your paddle, and using your arm strength *and* the weight of your body (not your back muscles), pull the paddle toward you.

To be a good forward paddler, you need not be a body builder. In fact, technique and teamwork are far more important than strength. At the Nantahala World Whitewater Rafting Championship, the U.S. All-Women's team took second place overall, not so much because of their strength but because of their style and technique. They worked well together. For this reason they were able to beat more than twenty all-male teams in slalom, downriver, and safety events.

### THE BACK PADDLE STROKE

A "back paddle!" command is given to tell everyone in the boat to perform a back stroke (Figure 6-2) together. To make a back stroke, lean forward, insert the paddle in the water behind you, and, using your hip or the side of the boat as a fulcrum or pivoting point, lean back.

## WOMEN IN RIVER RUNNING

I rarely know what to say or write when asked to comment on being a woman river runner. I grew up in a family and community where girls could do anything they wanted, whether it was cooking and sewing or running rivers and climbing mountains. Since I wasn't a very good cook, I was attracted to and stuck with the outdoor life.

In my twenty years of running rivers around the globe, I've witnessed some amusing incidents. In 1989 I worked as a raft guide on the Zambezi River in Africa, where macho South African men ruled the waters. When I showed up, they scoffed at the American girl who came to work on their mighty river, but lightened up when they saw how many push-ups I could do. They downright got quiet when I consistently was able to keep the boat upright better than they could. Then there was a time on Cherry Creek—a Class V run in California where many test their mettle—when a canoeist from the East Coast with a strong southern drawl said, "Heck, if a girl can do this, I can." He proceeded to swim his way down the river. By the end of the day he had to confess that maybe there was a girl out there who was just little better.

Advice for women and girls starting out: Be tenacious, be aggressive, be a team player. Know that it's OK to be scared, but don't let that fear stand in your way.

—Rypins, captain, U.S. Women's Whitewater Team

**Direction of Current**

*Figure 6-2*

## Back paddle

This stroke may take a bit more practice than the forward stroke, but once mastered it can be as effective as a good forward stroke.

### TURNS

Knowing how to respond to the commands of "right turn!" and "left turn!" is simple if you remember the following: The paddlers on the side of the boat that the command refers to always back paddle. In other words, when a guide calls "right turn!" (Figure 6-3) everyone on the right side of the boat back paddles; the left side forward paddles. In a "left turn!" (Figure 6-4) the left side of the boat back paddles; the right side of the raft forward paddles.

It is important that your bow paddlers understand what to do in the event of a "right turn!" or "left turn!" command, because the rest of the team will be following their examples. This should be practiced over and over at the beginning of every trip, especially if you have a new team of people paddling together for the first time.

There are different variants to the commands "right turn!" and "left turn!" Many guides break turns down into their components. For example, a "right turn!" becomes "right side back paddle, left side forward paddle!" It is really up to you whether to call a "right turn!" or a "right side back paddle, left side forward paddle!" when you're guiding. Both should produce the desired result of turning the boat

*Rafting*

*Figure 6-3*

**Right turn**

*Figure 6-4*

**Left turn**

**B A S I C   E S S E N T I A L S**

quickly to the right. I have found that the best commands are short, simple, and clear.

### STOP!

Guides often neglect the "stop!" command, even though it is as important as the other commands. "Stop!" means stop paddling. It does not mean that the team should stop the movement of the boat. "Stop!" means the team should take their paddles out of the water and be ready for the next command.

When you're guiding, use "stop!" to put your team into psychological "neutral" between commands. If possible, call out "stop!" in between every two linked commands. This allows your team to smoothly and quickly make a transition from one stroke to another, and helps to avoid confusion. For instance, your team is paddling forward and you decide that a right turn is needed. Instead of calling "forward!" immediately followed by "right turn!", insert a "stop!" in between: "Forward!", "stop!", "right turn!" This breaks the sequence just long enough for the team to be mentally and physically prepared for the next command. Getting in the habit of using the "stop!" command will help you become a more effective paddle guide.

## *The Draw and Pry Strokes*

There are two more advanced paddle strokes—the draw and the pry. Usually these are taught to a crew only after they have mastered the five basic commands. However, it is important that the guide know these strokes because they help to set and control the angle of the paddle boat.

The draw stroke (Figure 6-5) is used to make quick pivots or to move the boat sideways. It is used most often when the guide wants to make slight adjustments in the direction the boat is moving. To do a draw stroke, lean out away from the boat, put the paddle in the water at a right angle to the boat, and "draw" the boat toward the paddle. A draw stroke is easier to understand if you envision it as a "sideways" forward stroke. Do all the same things as you would during a forward stroke, only do them at a right angle to the boat.

The pry stroke (Figure 6-6) is the opposite of the draw stroke. To do a pry stroke, use the boat or your hip as a fulcrum or pivoting point and push the paddle out at a right angle to the boat. This stroke also is used most often by the guide to make slight corrections to the angle that the boat is moving along. A pry stroke is easier to understand by envisioning it as a "sideways" back stroke. Do all the same things as you would during a back stroke, only do them at a right angle to the boat.

To practice your guiding skills, take a raft out on a calm stretch of water. Using only your paddle and a pry stroke, turn the raft in one

**Direction of Raft**

*Figure 6-5*

**Draw stroke**

**Direction of Raft**

*Figure 6-6*

**Pry stroke**

full revolution and stop it with a draw stroke so that the raft points directly downstream. Then try it in the other direction using a draw stroke for the turn and stopping the raft using only a pry stroke. Use your paddle team to make the turn, then stop the raft so that it points directly downstream with either a draw or a pry, whichever is appropriate. This is a great way to get a feel for the boat and your ability.

## *Rigging a Paddle Boat*

One of the most attractive parts of paddle boating is that you don't need much equipment besides the boat, paddles, and a team to go downstream. Generally, paddle boats don't carry much excess gear; the food and camp gear is usually rigged onto an oar boat where it is easily stored. However, gear can also be rigged onto self-bailing rafts. Soft bags can be tied directly to the grommets on the floor without difficulty.

Specific rigging accessories for a paddle boat should include foot cups (Figure 6-7) glued to the floor. Foot cups are an innovation that provide paddlers with greater stability. Having your foot slide into a cup can help keep you in the boat—especially in big waves or when you're reaching for a sweeping draw stroke in turbulent water. An

*Figure 6-7*

**A foot cup**

important safety point to remember, however: Do not ever use foot cups in which your foot can in any way become stuck. In the event of a flip, you do not want to be stuck to the boat.

## *Paddle Boat Safety*

It used to be thought that paddle boats couldn't run difficult rivers. Many believed that the crews would fall out of the boat, leaving the guide with an empty boat that would be impossible to control alone. Now this belief is changing. It has become clear that a good paddle boat team can descend even the most difficult rivers safely—more safely than an oar boat in many cases—with a few very simple considerations.

First, and perhaps most important, become the best possible team you can be. Know each other's abilities. Know how to communicate with each other. Practice paddling together. Second, remember SAFETY always. For example, take care when swinging those paddles around in a rapid—a whack on the head is no fun. Third, don't get in over your head. Before you go out on the river, do your research: Become familiar with your commercial outfitter, the difficulty of the river, and your ability to deal with an emergency.

# Oar Boat Technique

The oar boat is a uniquely personal affair. Unlike the paddle guide who has a crew to help out, the oar guide has to do it all: Read the river, identify the obstacles, decide on the course of action, and execute that decision by rowing the boat solo. With the advent of self-bailing rafts and catarafts, "swampers" were no longer needed on an oar boat to bail water, making the guide the only person absolutely necessary aboard.

The oar guide sits on a seat in the middle of the boat and faces downstream. Unlike traditional rowboats that have the bow behind the guide, whitewater oar boats are turned around with the bow in front so that the guide will turn around backwards deliberately in a rapid, but most of the time the guide faces downstream.

To row you need a boat, a frame, and three oars. The oars attach to a frame, which is in turn attached to a boat. Oars come in many shapes and sizes, and the bigger the boat, the bigger the oar. A 22-foot snout-rig raft uses 13-foot counter-balanced oars that weigh over 60

## Figure 6-8

**An oar-powered raft with thole pins and clips**

pounds each, while 12-foot rafts may use 7-foot plastic oars that
weigh only 10 pounds each. Oars made for whitewater tend to be
strong and durable. However, there are many situations that will snap
even the most durable oar like a toothpick. This is why you should
always carry a spare oar on your boat. So many oars get broken on
the Zambezi River that every oar boat on every one-day trip there
carries 2 spare oars.

Oars are attached to frames by one of two systems: a pin and clip
or an oarlock. The pin and clip system (Figures 6-8 and 6-9) has a
fixed clip attached to the oar. This clip slides snugly over a pin that is
screwed into the frame. This system has the advantage and
disadvantage of permanently setting the oar's blade position. The
advantage of a set oar position is that every time you pull the oar, the
blade's angle relative to the water's surface will be just the way you
want it. At the same time, a set oar position can be a disadvantage
because if a fixed oar hits a rock, it may "pop" off the pin. Not only
does this render the oar useless until it is put back on the pin, but a
flying, loose oar can cause a lot of pain if it hits you.

*Figure 6-9*

The pin and clip system

*Figure 6-10*

The oarlock system

The other system to attach oars to frames is with traditional oarlocks and stoppers. This oarlock system (Figure 6-10) is versatile yet tricky. A stopper is fixed to the oar, which keeps the oar from sliding too far in the oarlock. Because the oars are free to rotate in the locks, if you lose your grip the angle of the oar blade relative to the water's surface can change. If this happens, the oar is said to be "feathered" in the water. A feathered oar is useless since it will easily slice through the water instead of "grabbing" it and propelling the boat. This is the disadvantage to an oarlock system. On the positive side, like using a stick shift in a car, which gives you better handling on the road, an oarlock system gives you a better "feel" of the water. To sum this up: Oarlocks are temperamental but responsive.

## *The Pull*

The pull (Figure 6-11) is a powerful stroke. To do a pull stroke, lean forward, put your oars in the water, transfer the power to your legs, and heave backwards. Lift your oars out of the water and begin again. Properly executed, even a small person can make a heavy boat move in a rapid. The pull stroke is the most popular and strongest stroke that you can make with an oar boat. Technique here is very important—even more important than strength. Use your entire body,

*Figure 6-11*

**The pull**

not just your arms. If you feel the pull in your legs, you're probably rowing the right way.

## *The Push or Portagee*

The portagee (Figure 6-12) is the opposite of the pull. To do this stroke, put your oars in the water, push forward, lift them out, and repeat. This stroke requires far more strength than does the pull stroke. Compared to the pull stroke, where much of the leverage and power come from the legs, portageeing requires much more upper body strength. Because so much upper body strength is used when pushing the oars, this is generally not as strong a stroke. Therefore, the portagee is not used as much as the pull. However, in recent years many top oarsmen have begun to advocate "pushing" down the river. Much more aggressive than pulling back, pushing allows you to maintain momentum through rapids.

## *The Double Oar Turn*

Just like a paddle boat, an oar boat turns quickest when one oar pulls back at the same time that the other pushes forward. For example, to make a right turn, the oar guide pulls on the right oar at the same time he or she pushes on the left. A quick pivot to the right

*Figure 6-12*

**The push or portagee**

results. Practice this turn until it is automatic. Many novices learn to turn by pulling only one oar, and they pick up this one-oar habit. Learn from the beginning to do *double oar* turns every time you turn—you'll be able to guide and control an oar boat much better if you do.

### Other Oar Phenomena

"Decking" or "shipping" an oar is what you do when there isn't enough room to fit the boat and fully extended oars through a tight spot. To deck an oar, quickly move the oar blade parallel to the boat. After you are past the tight spot, you are ready to swing your oars back into the water and begin rowing again.

### Rigging an Oar Boat

Oar boats are workhorses. Their heavy-duty frames can and usually do carry the bulk of the gear on a river trip. Everything from first-aid and repair supplies to personal dry bags, coolers of food, lawn chairs, commissary boxes, and portable toilets is carried on the oar boat. The main consideration when rigging an oar boat is to keep the heavy and hard gear low, the light and soft gear high. Above all, rig for a flip: tie everything onto the boat; use two lines if you can. When I flipped in a big wave in Hance Rapid on the Colorado River, I had neglected to tie more than one line across a cheese cooler in the front of my oar boat. All I can say is that there must be some fat, happy, cheese-stuffed fish at the bottom of that rapid.

### Oar Boat Safety

Because oar boats carry so much hard gear such as oars, frames, and metal boxes, take care to always wear a helmet when on an oar boat. Also, be sure to rig the boat so that the oars have a free range of motion. Many a knuckle has been smashed against many a cooler that was rigged too close to the oar stroke's path. Finally, watch the downstream oar when rowing. If this oar hits a rock, it may "pop" out and hit you. This is another good reason to always wear a helmet.

# Cataraft Technique

Catarafts can either be rowed or paddled, depending on the rig. Therefore, the techniques described above for maneuvering oar and paddle boats apply to catarafts. Strokes designed for kayaks and canoes are also often used since catarafts are so light and maneuverable.

In Russia, where the paddling cataraft originated, one popular design enables paddlers to kneel on the cataraft's tubes while paddling. Kneeling is tough on the legs but provides much greater leverage for strong, powerful strokes. As the use of catarafts for rafting has only recently begun to catch on here in the United States, there is still much to be learned about paddling cataraft technique. Unfortunately, if you want to try this exciting new river craft, you may have a very difficult time finding a commercial outfitter or whitewater school that uses catarafts. Instead, you may have to find someone with a cataraft to borrow, or buy one yourself.

# PLANNING A TRIP

O K, so now you're ready to go rafting. But where? With whom? What else do you need? No basic book would be complete without a discussion on how to plan an expedition. The first consideration is whether to hire the services of a guide or to strike out on your own. Until you have attended a whitewater school and have learned the skills with experts, I suggest that you use the services of a professional river outfitter. Later, after you have learned and practiced the skills, you can organize your own expedition. This chapter covers both possibilities.

## Commercial Trips

On a commercial rafting trip, you hire an outfitter to provide an experienced river guide to lead you and your friends down a river. The advantage to a commercial trip is that you don't need as much experience, and the outfitter usually provides almost all the necessary equipment. These trips allow budding rafters to get their get wet, so to speak, by providing a safe, exciting wilderness adventure without committing them to the major purchases of a boat and accessories. And for those who are not accustomed to "roughing it," a guided river trip is a perfect option since outfitters usually devote a great deal of effort to make their clients feel at home in the great outdoors. Exciting whitewater, breathtaking scenery, fresh air, plenty of good food, and interesting people make river running one of the fastest-growing sports today.

All in all, one of the best things about a commercial river trip is that it's easy. You don't need to be a river expert. You don't have to do a lot of planning yourself. You can pick up a phone any time and reserve a spot to float down some of the most spectacular rivers in the world. Everything from half-day, easy Class II float trips near your home, to three-week, Class V exploratories in Siberia are available by using the services of river outfitting companies.

Some guided river trips conduct "eco-tours" to endangered rivers throughout the world to call attention to the environmentally harmful dams planned there. In short, many commercial tours are more than a fun ride down a river; they are educational tools that give everyone an opportunity to develop a deeper understanding of our planet and its people.

Commercial river trips cost from $60 to $300 per day, depending on the river's difficulty, logistical complexity, and the number of guides needed to run the trip. On a charter trip, an outfitter will customize an itinerary for you or your group, for a price. However, if you sign up for a regular commercial trip, you must follow their itinerary. Except in the case of whitewater schools, you will not be responsible for guiding a boat yourself if you head down the river with a commercial outfitter. Consequently, commercial trips are especially appropriate if you are a beginner rafter.

Choosing a commercial trip means choosing a river and an outfitter. In deciding on an outfitter you should ask these questions: How long has the company been in business? Do they operate under permit by a government agency? What is their safety record? What are the guides' qualifications? It pays to do a little research before you choose your outfitter. Don't hesitate to ask questions.

## The Private Trip

After you have learned to guide and want to strike out on your own, you will then organize a private trip. First, decide which river to run. Guide books and river maps are available describing location, length, difficulty, river flows, and other pertinent information for most runnable rivers in the United States. Go to your local outdoor store and see what literature is available. Once you've chosen the river, make a packing list and a food menu.

## Shuttles

At some point you will need to think about arranging the shuttle-transportation such that you can reunite with your vehicle at the end

## SAMPLE PACKING LIST

**One-day Trips**
Raft
Frame
3 oars
3 oarlocks/pins and clips
Paddles
Pumps
Bow and stern lines
Throw bags
Webbing
Safety hardwear
First-aid kit
Repair kit
Water containers
Dry bag for clothing
Dry container for food

**Multiday Trips**
Camping gear

Personal dry bags
Waterproof containers with food
Firepan

Stove and fuel
Water containers
Pots and pans
Eating utensils
Water purification system

**Personal Gear**
Shorts
River sandals or shoes
Booties
Lifejacket
Helmet
Wet suit/dry suit
Paddle jacket/dry top
Polypropylene undergarments

of the trip without undo hassles. Depending on the river, shuttles may take many hours, so you need to plan for them. Some questions to consider are: How will you and the equipment get to the river? Where will you leave the car? Is it safe? How will you get back to it after the trip? Many popular rivers have shuttle services available; consult your guidebook or local whitewater club.

If you decide to run your own shuttle, use your imagination—some very imaginative solutions are possible. Bicycles, motorcycles, houseboats, hitchhiking, trains, and running shoes can all assist in reuniting everyone with their vehicles. In Russia, where few people have cars and few rivers are close to roads anyway, river rafters put everything in their backpack—food, on-river clothes, off-river clothes, sleeping gear, and boat. Often weighing upwards of 90 pounds, these backpacks are hiked up and over big, steep ridges to get to and from inaccessible rivers. This practice hasn't yet caught on in the United States. A semi-truck is needed to carry food and equipment for the average Grand Canyon expedition. One great advantage to the Russian "down-and-dirty" approach is that it solves the shuttle problem.

*Rafting*

# River Food

Depending on the length and difficulty of your river trip and how much space and weight you want to conserve, meal planning is either simple or complex. Everything from Spam, crackers, and instant coffee at each meal to a gourmet's delight that rivals the best French restaurant is possible. It completely depends your willingness to plan, purchase, and ultimately, carry the food. Oar boats are a great asset because they can hold a well-stocked, varied supply of tasty food and drink. However, an expedition that expects to portage a section of the river will only take a small amount of very light food, so there is less to carry. There are a number of very good wilderness cookbooks available that will give you some menu ideas.

# Permits

Many rivers in the United States are open to rafters only by special permit. Often flowing through the last remaining wilderness areas left on our planet, whitewater rivers are special places. It has become necessary for government agencies to regulate the use of whitewater rivers to protect them. Rivers have become such popular recreation areas for rafters, fishermen, campers, and swimmers that the government is determined to keep land use and its impact on the wilderness under control. Enter the permit system.

In the United States, the forest and park services as well as other local agencies regulate river use. Be sure to check whether you need a permit to run the river you have chosen. Some popular rivers have a long waiting list and can take up to five years (such as the Colorado in the Grand Canyon) for a permit. Most rivers, however, are less traveled and the only requirement you must fulfill is to go to the local regulating agency and pick up a permit the day you want to start.

# The Multiday Trip

Generally multiday trips (Figure 7-1) require far more planning than simple one-day outings. Not only do you need a boat, safety gear, paddles, lifejackets, first-aid supplies, a repair kit, and lunch, but you must also bring tents, tarps, sleeping bags, clothes, cooking gear, more food, and a porta-potty. Planning a long, extended rafting trip becomes down-right complicated.

Consider also that multiday, wilderness river trips require a greater

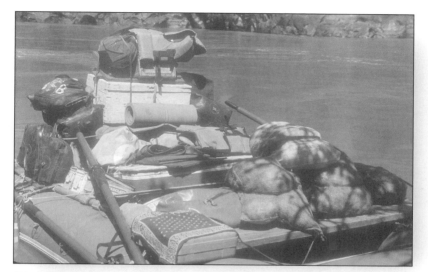

*Figure 7-1*

**Careful planning and ample equipment are required for a multiday trip**

level of commitment and corresponding competency of the guides. Usually, the longer the trip, the farther away you will be from a road or help should an emergency occur. Think about the safety issues of the river you want to run. Know what to do in an emergency before you head off on the river.

As a beginner, don't be wary of going on a long river trip with competent guides. It is well worth the effort. After a few days all the things that seem so important or pressing when you are at home will start to fade. The stresses of your fast-paced life will melt as you begin to mesh with the natural cycle of river time. I definitely recommend going on a long trip, but go with a commercial outfitter your first time. Observe their systems, ask questions, learn how to rig those big boats. And above all, enjoy!

## River Trips Around the World

If you want to explore new and exotic rivers, I recommend that you go with a reputable outfitter who has experience with the intricacies of international travel. If you choose to run the gauntlet by yourself (and sometimes you'll end up running the gauntlet with an outfitter since you can't count on *anything* going exactly as planned on an international river trip), be prepared to deal with everything in this book *plus* visas, international air tickets, overweight baggage, customs fees, language difficulties, potentially unreliable domestic transportation, strange food, poor maps, and some of the most exotic and spectacular places left on the planet.

Two great international outfitters are Bio Bio Expeditions (800-260-RAFT) and Sobek Expeditions (800-282-8747).

There is no question that one of the ultimate adventures is to run a river in a faraway land. It provides access to places and people that can't be experienced any other way. On every continent except Antarctica, whitewater rivers have been explored and investigated. For the modern explorers among us, international river exploration is an experience not to be missed.

# THE RIVER AS A METAPHOR

S o there you have it. A primer on the basic essentials of rafting. A
small book on the how-to's and where-with-all's of this exciting
sport. If I've done my job, now you can safely and quickly learn to
raft. However, in addition to everything discussed in the previous
chapters, I must address one more essential that to me is absolutely key.
While less tangible than the others, this one is just as important.

It has been said that life is a river. And indeed, as a metaphor for
life I know none better. Life is a magical journey into the unknown.
So, too, is a river trip. One never knows what lies around the next
bend. Problems will need to be overcome; obstacles will need to be
avoided. Fighting against the current doesn't work. Neither does
merely floating along. No, it takes courage and passion to approach
the wildness of the river. To feel its life surging downstream and to
feel its magic is to know what it is to live.

Sometimes calm, sometimes chaotic, the river holds incredible
opportunities for personal growth—if one simply pays attention.
Some good practices, both on the river and off:

1. Stay out of holes. Try to avoid getting stuck.

2. When something bad happens, don't ask, "How did I get
here?" or "Who's at fault?" Rather, ask, "Where am I?" and "How
do I get to where I want to go?"

3. Stop and scout whenever you can't see the bottom. Take
your time.

4. If things get too difficult, portage.

*Figure 8-1*

**Rafters in the Bio Bio River in Chile**

*Figure 8-2*

**A rafting trip down a river can be a wild experience**

5. From time to time, eddy out, rest, and enjoy the scenery.

6. Marvel in the wonder of our magical planet. Appreciate that you are part of a flow that actually goes much deeper than the surface currents that you observe in your everyday life.

7. If you are overly concerned with getting to the bottom (or to the top, as the case may be), you'll miss what is going on all around you. Remember to experience the ride as you go along.

8. Always choose your route. However, if you hit a rock, be flexible enough to change directions if necessary.

These are just some of the practices I recommend on the river, as in life. Bottom line, it all comes down to respect—for the river, the planet, and life. People sometimes wonder why I've spent so much of my life visiting rivers, rafting down rivers, swimming in rivers. It's because of how much I learn there—not only about the river and its environs, but also about myself and others.

I invite you to use what you have learned from this book to go run a river. Sometimes it may be cold, dark, and wet, and you may have a hard time breathing. Other times you will experience your life like you never have before. The most wonderful rewards can be found in the *process* of going down the river, regardless of how far you go or where you end up when it's all over. Enjoy!

# INDEX